100-Year-Old Animals

by Janet Stutley

Table of Contents

Chapter 1
Which Animals Live for a Long Time?

Many animals can live for a long time. Scientists confirm that rhinos can live for up to 40 years. That is a long time, but some animals live longer.

A rhinoceros looks old. But it cannot live as long as some other animals. ⊕

⋔ An elephant also looks old. But it cannot live for more than 70 years.

Elephants can live for almost 70 years.

That is a long time, but some animals live even longer.

Female orca whales can live for up to 80 years.

⬇ Orca whales can jump.

That is also a long time. But some animals can live for more than 100 years.

Each pod of orca whales makes its own calls or sounds. ↻

Chapter 2

How Long Do Giant Tortoises Live?

Giant tortoises can live for more than 150 years. They seem ancient.

Giant tortoises live on Galapagos Islands, near South America. ⏻

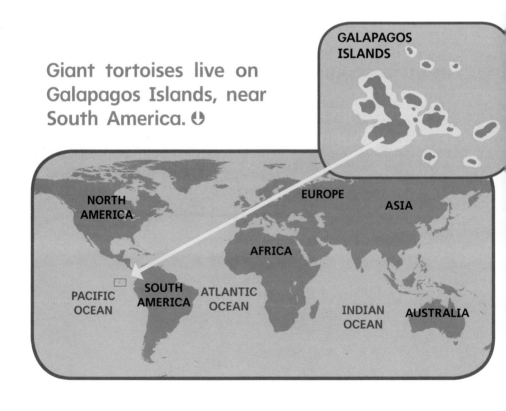

People are hopeful that giant tortoises will stay safe on the Galapagos Islands. ↻

Some people used to hunt giant tortoises. They move slowly. They were easy to catch.

You cannot hunt tortoises now.

Chapter 3

How Long Do Whale Sharks Live?

The whale shark can live for up to 100 years. The whale shark is a kind of shark. It is not a whale.

This whale shark lives in the ocean near Australia.

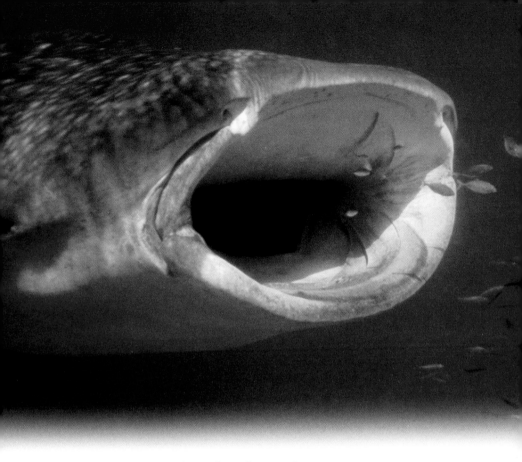

⊙ A whale shark swims near
the top of the ocean to eat.

Whale sharks open their mouths as they swim. That is how they catch tiny sea animals to eat.

⌂ It is safe for divers to swim with whale sharks.

Whale sharks are the biggest fish in the world.

Whale sharks move slowly. They swim about as fast as people walk.

Chapter 4

How Long Do Giant Clams Live?

Scientists say that some giant clams can live for 100 years. Giant clams live in warm waters.

↻ Most giant clams live near colorful coral reefs.

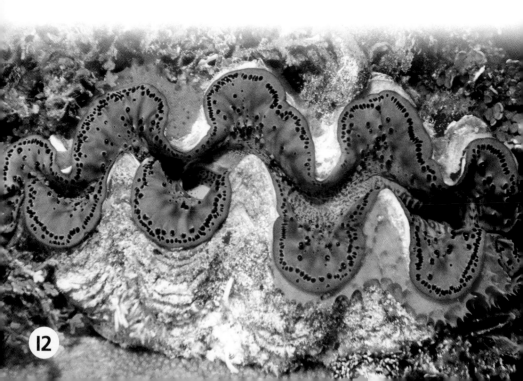

Some giant clam shells grow more than four feet (1.3 m) long. This clam shell is almost half that size. ⮕

A giant clam has a soft body inside a shell.

Giant clams are unable to move.
They just open and close
their shells.

↺ This giant clam shell is open. An animal
may have eaten the clam inside.

⌒ The giant tortoise, giant clam, and whale shark can live for more than 100 years.

No one knows why some animals live so long. One valid guess may be their slow movements. They spend a lot of time resting.

Comprehension Check

Retell

Use the photos to help you retell the information in this book.

Think and Compare

1. Turn to pages 10 and 11. What did you learn about whale sharks? *(Summarize)*

2. Which animal in this book would you like to see up close? Why? *(Analyze)*

3. Why is it helpful for scientists to know how long an animal can live? *(Evaluate)*